GROW WILD

GROW WILD

Poetry for Hurting and Healing Hearts

LAUREN FRIEDAUER

RESOURCE *Publications* • Eugene, Oregon

GROW WILD
Poetry for Hurting and Healing Hearts

Resource Publications
An Imprint of Wipf and Stock Publishers
199 W. 8th Ave., Suite 3
Eugene, OR 97401

www.wipfandstock.com

PAPERBACK ISBN: 978-1-6667-1947-5
HARDCOVER ISBN: 978-1-6667-1948-2
EBOOK ISBN: 978-1-6667-1949-9

08/11/21

Dedicated to Ethan Kuhlmann, a fellow worker of words.
For helping me believe I was capable.

the dead

the dead

i am afraid of the five minutes of silence before i fall asleep.
i cannot bear to be alone with my thoughts, even if they aren't bad.
am i afraid to be alone or afraid of myself?

how did you ever think your hands would be stable enough?

how did you think your fists could turn into open palms?

you are not soft and gentle

those words have never followed your name

you are the volatility of shaking heartbeats

scattered lightning storms

and messy teenage bedrooms.

you are a mosaic put together in the wrong way

how did you ever think someone could find that endearing?

your hands spill red paint red blood red hurt

naive and foolish

the waves of your fingerprints are covered in things you didn't do right and things you could have done better.

how did you ever think God would have time for you?

you are the smudged lead of a mistake the pencil couldn't quite erase completely.

you are the one building standing on feeble foundational knees left untouched by the damage of war.

a war you also created.

how did you ever think you could stop raining fire and instead rain water?

maybe all those things he said about you were right.

and what about your tongue?

how did you ever think you wouldn't bite?

you're a snake

cunning and manipulative and wrapping your way

around limbs of victims

then snake turned puppeteer

nailing strings into skin and yanking them this way and that.

how did you ever think you could be any different?

the dead

anxiety is soul crushing
this is a lightning storm i haven't ever felt before
i'm drowning
i forgot how to breathe
forgot how to swim
and i'm sinking
scrambling like there are footholds for me to hold onto
but all i am is surrounded by ocean
no footholds here
just water and my own fear
i am going to die

Grow Wild

shaking hands
there are whipping twisters in my lungs
and i can't really breathe anymore
i forgot what it's like to breathe
my hands are tearing my skin apart
in an attempt to pry my ribs open
because maybe if i spill my entire being out
i'll be able to feel like i have enough space inside of me.
cause that's what this feels like
all of my insides have grown too big for my body
i am being crushed from the inside out
my own body is trying to kill me
and i have no say over it

i am made with the intention
of perfection
but somewhere along the way
i touched the pan when i was told not to
i caught my hand between door and frame
i'm sorry dad i was naive to think i was indestructible
i'm sorry dad but my fingers are twisted crooked
and the way i touch things now is distorted
if the key wont fit
i'll make the lock fit
and i bend what shouldn't be bent
because i'm desperate to make something or someone fit
i just want someone to hold my hand

Grow Wild

i know what it's like to carry everybody's worlds on my shoulders
i have been burdened by my own heart
caring too much about everything and everyone
i see you dragging your feet
and fall to my knees to help you pick them up
lift your heels a little higher
your back curves into a slouch
share some of your
maybe all of your weight with me
i will clip my wings
to let other birds fly

the dead

are you awake right now?
my darkness is whispering to me again

Grow Wild

this is wolf territory

it looks like flickering fluorescents

or street lamp posts glowing sickly

or cavernous alleyways with simple moonlight

wolf territory is dangerous

for they are hungry

hungry and rabid

with souls that look like shadows and knives and barbed wire

they are crooked grins

snapping yellow teeth

bent out of shape claws that snag on your clothes

or maybe your skin if they're quick enough

quick enough to snatch you when your guard is down

and when you lose your white knuckle grip on the keys between
your fingers

or maybe when the fear turns dangerously cold and freezes your
bones into brittle

if you don't move he might not see you

he might not touch you where he shouldn't

he might not bite you where he shouldn't

fight flight or freeze

nobody told you about the ice

wolf territory is dangerous

you know

do not give them anything to grab onto

do not make it easier for them

they say

everybody says

maybe we should be domesticating these wolves instead

turning them into dogs

raising them into dogs
that don't bite
that know not to bite
so then you and i
her and i
don't have to leave the house
with fear clinging to our backs
gargoyle style
fanned out wings and stone talons
heavy and sharp and painful
because wolf territory is dangerous

Grow Wild

sometimes i feel like i am only made up of my skeleton
crooked bones bent out of shape
there are cracks everywhere in their dusted alabaster
and sometimes these bones feel sucked dry of marrow and calcium
they are brittle and made of dry sand

i am covered in someone else's fingerprints
HIS fingerprints
it doesn't matter who HE is
HE is all of them
all of the hands that didn't know what they were doing
and all of the ones that did
especially those ones
the hands that touched me everywhere they shouldn't have
mind heart soul
body
why couldn't you have just kept to yourself?

HIS hands
full of rage and pride and insecurity and a deep starvation of love
so HE took mine without asking
and now sometimes i can't stand in front of God with these shaking
knees

i am emaciated
my skin stretching over my ribs
i am anxious and on edge
deer in headlights
taut muscles ready to jump
ready to run

the dead

the worst part of it all
i feel used
does HE only want me for the limbs and the skin and muscles and
breasts and stomach and everything in between
ugly spider limbs and pale sickly skin and weak muscles and small
breasts and too thin too small too anything
she doesn't understand
i hate the way i look
stretched out and worn down and used and repeated and tattered
somebody else's toy before YOURS
i feel used
why doesn't HE love me for my heart,
and not just the shell that contains it?
i feel manipulated
it's okay for HIM to breathe on you like this
for HIM to peel you apart like this
for HIM to leave you empty and for dead like this

the worst part of the worst part
i feel unwanted and unlovable
this loneliness is swelling
it feels like a balloon sitting between my ribs
squeezed and stretched tight
i'm trying to feel it
trying to be okay with it
nothing's really working

Grow Wild

an unhealthy cycle of
werewolf evenings
where i've started sitting on my bed
knee to knee with the devil
who looks very much like me with
a wider grin and sharper teeth and darker eyes
but still very much me
these werewolf evenings are full of
black anger
and the devil reminding me of all the things i don't have
it's getting harder to keep him out
i've stopped trying and now i've stopped wanting to try
and repeat
and repeat
and repeat

the dead

a restless heart feels like
wherever your feet stand
is not good enough
they are buried in sand instead of
pressed against rock
i don't want to fall asleep
because i don't want tomorrow to rise
but i can't stop the earth from turning
the sun from changing guard with the moon.
the change will come no matter what.
don't waste energy trying to stop it.
it will only break you.

Grow Wild

it is not poetic
it is not simple
i cannot turn it into a metaphor
that makes me feel better
it is not the
forest fires or tsunamis or earthquakes
it is the quiet
the few hours just before dawn
when the whole world is asleep
except for it
the muffled bubbling of water in your ears
after you dunk your head underwater
and the dull screaming of your lungs when you've held your breath
for too long
it is restless
the tossing and turning in bed sheets that itch at your skin
a tension in your chest
like someone squeezing their fingers around your heart so tightly
that their nails leave marks
and all you wanna do is scream
but it is quiet
it steals your breath
and your heartbeat
and your voice
until suddenly you don't think your entire body could make an-
other sound ever again
maybe it's better this way

she calls me to confess someone else's sin
i am reminded of the way my body was robbed from me
by hands that had no intention of being kind
she does not deserve this darkness
when i tell her speaking from experience
it feels as though i'm just passing my demons off to her
hold the leash and be careful
they like to bite the places that hurt most
this is something i don't want to share
she shouldn't have to know what it's like to have your skin taken
from you without permission

Grow Wild

please let go of me
i am tired of feeling your fingers curl around my rib cage
tired of feeling the fear you breathe into my lungs
the anxiety you shake into my bones
you are smaller than me
this i know
but you run around my feet with a hammer
and smash my knees into pieces
and then you pull my hair until i'm down with you
our noses touch
and you say to me

"you aren't worth loving. they only look at you because you're
pretty, not because you have anything to offer. they only touch you
because of what they can get out of it. no one wants to love you they
just want to fuck you."

how crippling is that
and it's little at first and then it swallows me whole
and suddenly i am gone
eaten alive by these lies

please let go of me

the dead

i am struggling, Jesus
feeling picked clean again
Satan's skeleton claws twist at my ribs
and scratch around the cavern of my chest for my heart
he finds it easy
finds it and covers it and whispers on it
and he tells me all these things

you are worthless
you are just your body and nothing else
you don't deserve to be loved for anything more than the shell you
came in
you are used and dirty and ugly and no one wants you
you are too skinny
you are too broken

can you hear me, Jesus?
i know you can
all i want is safety
sometimes i feel like i'm drowning
please rescue me my feet are slipping my hands are shaking my
heart is beating faint my head is pounding thunder
i cannot cry any louder because someone has his hands around my
throat

i can't get rid of feeling tattered
hand-me-down five times
stretched out and faded like denim worn too much
i can't get rid of feeling like somebody else's

Grow Wild

this safety is a foreign concept to me
i am used to being
used
to the way hands that aren't mine cover me
i can look in the mirror and see where it happened
where this daughter of God was mishandled
they are handprints of red paint
or maybe it's blood
but certainly not theirs
it's mine
it's always mine

here i am
in my bathroom
and i lay my own shaking hands across the divots in my body
i wonder what man would ever see this tatter as beautiful
i wonder about the daughter i might have and then i'm afraid for her

this is where he tried to see if he could touch his forefinger and
thumb together around your neck
where he tried to make your throat smaller
maybe it was because he didn't want to hear you ramble on anymore
this is where he burned your knee through your jeans with his palm
where he burned through your fondness of taking the train by
yourself like paper
from those ashes came fear
this is where he stole your mouth with his in the back of a theater
and wouldn't stop poking his fingers into your body no matter how
many times you told him to stop
where you get anxious going to see movies with other boys because
you're trying to keep what little piece of yourself you have left
this is where he manipulated you and raped you

the dead

and where he didn't ask but told
where he laid claim to you

when you are already claimed
by hands that never take but give
by a love that redeems and heals and restores
by Him

why can't i feel it?
why can't i know it?

rescue me
i cannot do it without you, Jesus
please set me free and save me
this tired soul needs to rest

Grow Wild

redeem me.
help me my soul is broken
my heart is broken
my bones are broken
i am broken.
can you hear me?
you haven't spoken to me in months
i can't tell if you're listening anymore
but i will continue to cry out to you.
i am suffering.
the devil is pressing burning palms into my skin and i am melting.
please save me.
please rescue me.
he's killing me.
i'm killing me.

stayed up too late again
really searching my bones again
rattling my cup against my ribcage like a jailbird again.
feeling emaciated
stripped clean of my flesh and my muscles
when i crawl into bed I'm just my skeleton
and i catch my blanket's threads
i am starving
spider fingers stretching
reaching with infantile need
towards that Holy Light
my restless limbs
snagged marrow and calcium
and i'm tangled
stuck in the unintentionally sought out deprivation of love of patience of grace
He offers them to me
resting flat on His open palms of golden everything
something isn't letting me take it
this bed isn't letting me take it
MY bed isn't letting me take it
when i look again
i can see threads turn fingers
and despite how crooked and malformed they appear
they are recognizably mine.
my inner demon with her snarling teeth and hooked claws
her spiraling horns and burnt skin
with His Holiness set before me
i won't let me take it.
can't figure out why

want to know why

GOD HELP ME

MY BONES GROW WEARY

I NEED YOU I NEED YOUR STRENGTH

CAST HER OUT PRY HER FISTS FROM MY FLESH

FREE ME SET ME FREE I AM REACHING I AM REACHING
PLEASE MEET ME WHERE I'M AT PLEASE COME A LITTLE
CLOSER PLEASE HELP ME

SET ME FREE FROM THE JAILHOUSE OF MY RIBCAGE SET
ME FREE FROM THE RESTLESSNESS THE TANGLED SHEETS
THE FAMINE AND THE DESERT.

SET

ME

FREE

i'm running out of words to write

that match the disfigured cacophony in my chest

the cracked and rusted bells that echo against my warped bones

it sounds like the wilting song of a dying church

in an empty town

i'm inhabited by spirits now

made of once was

and almost

and not quite

it is hard not to wonder if it was the way i don't breathe between the words that i speak too loud

or the way my skeleton juts out of my skin

or the way my emotions sometimes run rampant like a team of spooked horses

it is hard not to listen to everything the Devil tells me

he likes to talk and he sounds like honey

sometimes he sounds like you

you know you've heard him before

he makes things lose their shape

bends daydreams into crooked nightmares

while convincing me that it was all my fault

that it was the fact that i am so unlovable

the color of red is a familiar one

the muted murmur in my being

after the dust settles,

it's always so hard to listen to the Life in my body

my fingers are searching though

the in between

white noise
that's all anything is
just constant noise
God bring me silence
i just want to hear your voice
help me to understand
i am desperate for anything besides a whisper
broken fingernails scratching at rock walls
i am trying to find the way out
God,
i beg of you to call me out of this cave
with fire and wind and lightning
i cannot see and i'm trying to

but you are a God of quiet murmurs
of stillness
breathe your voice into my ears
i will follow where you want me to go

God,
i am unequipped
i am unqualified
but i am called by you
so hand me my rod and staff
and go before me

whisper and i will follow
lead and i will follow

Grow Wild

God's voice speaks and the world shakes
thunder rattles the skeleton of this house
and the skeleton of this girl

heartbreak kid
with feet that haven't figured out
what it's like to stand still
don't move
with lungs that haven't figured out
what it's like to breathe quiet
don't gasp those wave crashing breaths
your chest could beat cliff-sides into submission
are you tired yet?
don't lie to me

heartbreak kid
are you tired of thunderstorms?
they live around your heart
and their lightning burns your bones
you are so angry
stop clenching your fists
your fingernails are cutting your own palms
open
your hands
and hold mine instead
the world does not hate you like you think it does
God does not hate you like you think He does
stop hating Him back
you are just chasing your own tail

heartbreak kid
rest a little
it is okay to not be okay

Grow Wild

you have a wild mind, my child
your imagination likes to run too far ahead of your logic
the only thing that can keep pace with it is your heart
the troublemakers
and then you're left with chaos all inside you
when there really isn't anything wrong

the in between

i have a bad habit of
holding onto things
so tightly that my knuckles turn white
holding onto things
that i should have let go of
a long time ago
until God has to pry my fingers from them
while saying
I HAVE SOMETHING SO MUCH BETTER FOR YOU

Grow Wild

there is a patience sitting in my bones
at the bottom of my stomach and my heart
slowly picking its way to the top
sometimes loving means waiting

sometimes i wish i could go back
i would tell the girl i used to be to stop
and maybe she would listen if she saw what her choices did to her
no i don't blame her
i wish she had been strong enough to say no
and maybe those moments would still be hers
and maybe she would still be able to decide who deserved them
i wish i could go back
i would tell her to choose someone else
i would tell her to choose herself

Grow Wild

these thunderstorms are familiar
reintroduce yourself to your anxiety and your fears
but don't let them get comfortable
don't allow them the opportunity to sit down
because they will make your body and your mind and your heart
their home.
they will infest you
latch onto the parts of you that keep you breathing
and drain you of your being.
don't give them the room to thrive.
make your light and your life big enough to squash them
take up room
take up space
give yourself permission to live

the in between

3:30 am
i am searching
digging for answers
like i am the paleontologist
and my heart is the desert.

3:32 am
there is poetry on the inside of my ribs,
your faded metaphors, comparisons to beauty.
i used to be able to read it
but now it's a foreign, ancient language
posted above the door of tombs.
i wonder if you still think i'm the beauty that you said i was,
buried treasure instead of a
rotting corpse.

3:35 am
deserts and tombs
with dinosaur bones and Egyptian mummies
are graveyards to paleontologists.

3:40 am
you loved grave robbing.

3:42 am
luckily, you found me
before my walls caved in.
you salvaged what you could.

Grow Wild

3:45 am
no.
wait.
you pillaged,
took what wasn't yours,
tried to wash your hands after

3:46 am
the dust of my bones
and blood of my body
is still on your fingertips.

3:50 am
by the time you finished,
my walls could barely stand.
they crumbled.
it's okay, though.
i took you down with me.

3:52 am
the dust is clearing and
i'm starting to find myself again.

3:53 am
my worth is not measured by how much gold i carry,
or how beautiful i am in the eye of the beholder.
my heart is the desert
it's dry and cracked
but it's hiding something amazing.
i don't need anyone else to tell me that.

this is the sound of heartbreak
she is tapping on my shoulder
knuckles on the door
of me trying to keep it all together
this is much softer
she calls my name sweetly
a simple breath
a simple whisper
and i haven't taken the step to let her inside
because i'm scared that she won't leave

but maybe i should let her in for a little bit

she knows that my heart is not her home
and she won't overstay her visit
so i will answer her
and offer her the couch in the living room
offer her all the places he touched
all the things he liked
all the words he said
and she will take them and turn them over in her hands
she will study them and maybe comment on them a little and then
she'll tell me to let it go

she will reminisce with me
and laugh with me
and cry with me
and get angry with me
feel with me
but she will always tell me to let it go

Grow Wild

i never have to ask her to leave

she does it on her own

when i don't notice it or

when i leave the room to do something else

she'll get up from the couch and slip out of my chest.

and then i'll come back to a fuller brighter room and forget she was
even there in the first place

i've seen your darkness
and i've seen the way you've climbed mountains
the dirt is under your fingernails
you're still climbing but you're almost there
let God carry you if he has to
you will make it you will summit

Grow Wild

i believe the human body is made with music
the foundation of skeletons and bones
molded together with symphonies that God wrote himself
He sang and we were born
that is why we feel music so deeply
songs and notes and chords
that weave deep into our inner being
mimic the heartbeat in our chests
it makes you want to move
makes you come alive
stokes the fire and breathes on the embers
and you are ignited
burning and dancing
there are orchestras in your lifeblood
let them sing

Heavenly Father

can You hear it? this pain is loud, it is deafening, sounds like rolling thunderstorms and this anxiety is the lightning. cracking in my bones, our bones, the children of tragedy. this anxiety sounds like gunshots and it feels like rattling skeletons turned earthquakes.

i know You can feel it too because it's raining

Heavenly Father

rescue me. rescue us.

rescue these shaking hands
this heart that beats like a kick drum
these hungry lungs
this tired mind
broken soul

Heavenly Father

take this lightning
take these thunderstorms

guide me to peace
guide me to comfort

surrender

Grow Wild

DAUGHTER

Father
take these anxious roaming hands into Yours

STILL YOUR BEATING HEART.

this heart has so many abnormalities
irregularities
war torn and bleeding
my skin red

LET ME WASH YOU CLEAN.

wild feet quit running
wild lungs quit heaving

I AM CALLING TO YOU. QUIET NOW.

listening
open palms
open ribs
open heart
closed eyes

curling toes in the sand
ocean swallowing my ankles
drown me in Your grace and mercy and love and forgiveness
drown me in Your heartbeat.

FOLLOW ME AND I WILL MAKE YOU NEW.

on my knees
roots sprouting from my bones
sinking into my faith
into You.
steady me
grow me
change me.

I WILL BRING GLORY TO YOUR SUFFERINGS.

i can feel it now
the sunlight inside of me
Your glory
holy glory

Father
DAUGHTER.

the lover

this is a love story about the sun and the moon
the sun
breathing fire and dancing light
she is energy
bringing life to others
sprouting flowers between ribs
the moon
sits still while the wind whistles through the trees in his chest
he is quiet and doesn't take up much space
calls the earth and all its creatures to still
their souls have known each other for ages
since god kissed the universe into existence
and when they touch
color explodes

Grow Wild

she leans into him with her lips stretched wide
this is a grin that beams adoration
and he lifts the back of his hand to her cheek
rests it on her jaw and rubs his thumb against her bottom lip
wiping something off i can imagine
maybe her lipstick smudged from a deep kiss
maybe he just wanted to touch her in an unconventional way
because love is unconventional
it breaks all the rules
it is chaotic and messy and life giving
even in the smallest touches
the private moments shared in public
when he rests his hand on her face
and she leans into him

the lover

intimacy

we strip each other down to our bare bones

the skeletons of our desires and dreams

the darkest corners of our insecurities and fears

you touch me in places no one ever has except for God

and it makes me think that He guides your hands

i have never explored the inner workings of another human being's everything

i know the carvings of your body, each ridge and divot

and i have memorized the pathways of your heart as if they were my own

this is a delicate discovery

we have peeled the layers of our flesh

dismantled the fear of being found out

let me tell you what i've found out

we shared bruised muscles and cracked sidewalks

sometimes uneven

but the sunlight we touch each other with floods these cracks with flowers and

the water we kiss each other with washes the bruises from our skin and suddenly

we are no longer afraid of being found out

Grow Wild

i saw two lovers on the train tonight
earbuds split between the two
and i thought of us

how can i communicate this to you
the abnormal beat-skipping in my chest
the kick drum forgetting when to come in
hitting twice and hitting loud just to make sure i'm listening
to the yanking of my sleeve
my heart has fingers curled tight around the fabric of my insides
and is pulling
pulling
pulling
this is it
and then i feel it all at once
soft midnight exchanges of words
the creation of a space without galaxies and stars and cosmos
save for the ones God weaved into your skin
there is breath at the nape of my neck
intimidating and exciting
sunrises that taste like eggs and bacon and your mouth
shared earbuds on trains for what i hope is eternity

i think i belong with you
when He made you,
God opened you up,
fished a rib from your chest,
and put it in mine.
your name is written on the bone
the lettering engraved
and each time my heart beats
they touch
i have been looking for you in other people
coming up empty handed and body fragmented
i was getting desperate
fingernails chipped and my being worn down to the bone
and then i met you
my brain did not know at first but my heart did
it recognized the touch of your name
and found it in those deep blue eyes
my soul knew
"this is who you are meant to love"
it whispered to me
and then when i touched you
laid my hands on your chest
i felt the shape of my rib beneath your skin
my name carved on the alabaster of bone
and i said to you
i think i belong with you

Grow Wild

i showed you all of my scars today
some of them are new flesh
sealed with kisses from heaven
some of them are still healing
jagged edges while the blood is still warm
and still dripping

i showed you all of them
pointed them on my body and told you
this is where the devil touched me
this is where i broke
bones not meant to break

i showed you my fear
the dog that nips at the back of my heels
and tells me secrets about you that not even you know
secrets that lie

but you touched me where the devil did
and it did not hurt
you pressed rose petals into my skin
and met heaven's lips with yours
and muzzled my fear
tied its jaws shut when you told me
you want me anyway
you love me anyway

the lover

kissing souls
this is what kissing souls looks like
it is laughter between pressed lips
deep belly
crinkled nose
pig snort
laughter
it is not taking ourselves too seriously
kiss me dry in this rain
make my heels kick up dust while your fingers turn my hips to yours
and when we touch
our souls do too
it is a sharing of skin and squeezing our space together
until it explodes all over us and paints us into galaxies
we are covered in starlight
untouchable
invincible
kissing souls is rubbing noses
accidentally bumping teeth and giggling
because it isn't supposed to be perfect
it is the way your jaw fits in my hands
and i know that when God designed you
when He carved your bones
He thought of my hands.
"this is where her fingers will go when she loves you and it will be
good," declares the Lord.
kissing souls is matching lungs and heart
breathing for each other
how lucky am i to be the one that feels your life beneath my palms
all butterfly wing rollercoaster stomachs

Grow Wild

all thunderstorm kick drum heartbeats

all ocean wave cliff crashing breaths

kissing souls is knowing you

not just the way your lips curl

or the freckle on your nose next to your eye

it is knowing your fears

and what hurts you most

and what makes you laugh hardest

kissing souls is cartography of the human heart

mapping the things that are bad and landmarking the things that are good.

it is messy and winding up and down and criss-crossing and sometimes more than one road leads to the same place

but

that's what kissing souls is

it is beautiful and it is slow and it is gentle and it is good

it's like keeping secrets
whispering to each other about the thoughts only God can hear
it's like coming home
like seeing the mountains for the first time after months without
them
my heart instantly settles among your forests
and damn how beautiful it all is
all your valleys and jagged edges and peaks
carved so specifically
so purposefully
it's to be breathless
and dizzying and on the tips of my toes
sometimes i feel like i can't keep up with you
but that doesn't stop me from trying
and it doesn't stop you from waiting
it's like the ocean
vast and unexplored
and i am anxious to dive deep below the surface
discover what no one ever has before
things you've kept in the darkest trenches for years
it's like wildflowers in the summer
or colorado sunsets
there is so much life and color
it's like meeting an old friend
my soul is familiar with yours
no amount of time can pass that we won't remember
it's how excited dogs get when the people they love come home
it's like taking your shoes off after a long day
and feeling the carpet twine between your toes
and i pray that it can be like this forever

loving a writer

i can turn you into metaphors and similes
turn your kisses into fresh rain
your eyes into the ocean
the way you loved me into coming home after being gone for so
long
into a deep breath
and i can turn our heartbreak into
thunderstorms and lighting
navy waves breaking apart cliffside
into melancholy mornings and bed sheets that trap me and i just
don't want to get up
i can say all these things
and write all this vague imagery
but when i strip it down and expose its simplicity
i love you
that's all it really is
and i will break my heart in two
if it means yours will beat

the lover

why do we call them good byes?
there's nothing good
about leaving you

Grow Wild

missing you feels a lot like
someone taking a pick axe to my skeleton
shattering my knee caps
chiseling away at the white until my legs and feet are
dust
it feels a lot like the ocean's powerful hands
sweeping me under its current
and holding me down until all the space inside me is full of water
by then my heartbeat is just a murmur

the lover

3:00 am
i've been speaking to the mountains

"what do they sound like?"
she asks me in the darkness of a room that isn't mine

well,
i tell her
their voices are deep
they set off earthquakes in my bones
they sound like standing in the bell tower of a church at noon
sweet and thick and harmonious
sometimes they whisper when they don't want to be heard
but for the most part
when they speak to me
they thunder
and it is slow and somber
a sort of weeping.

"what do you talk about? why are they crying?"
she asks me in the darkness of a room a thousand miles away

we talk about how much we miss you,
i say to her,
we talk about the echoes of you
footprints you left on their rocks
or the ones you left in my head
the smell of your perfume
the symphony of your voice and your heartbeat and your life
the blue curiosity of your eyes

Grow Wild

i tell them about the
touch of your lips
how my skin still burns where you kissed me
and they confess jealousy.

"i miss you too"
she whispers in the darkness that separates us

and the mountains cry

the lover

i notice the emptiness
of the space you used to occupy in this room
it is the heaviest thing i've ever shouldered
i wish you would have wanted to stay more
than you wanted to go

Grow Wild

i cannot dream without you in it
and i cannot decide
if it's a blessing
or a curse

i only think about you when certain songs come on.

i think about your hair and the untidiness to it.

i think about your heart and the untidiness to it.

that's just it, isn't it? there's an untidiness to you that i could never clean up, no matter how much i tried.

i only think about you when certain songs come on.

i always skip them.

the growth

the growth

advent

there is such a thing as complete darkness
darkness where your eyes can't adjust
there are no lights to turn on
no coming sun
and all you have is your hands
to touch whatever surrounds you
and your feet to guide you
but my feet are broken and
it hurts to move so i don't
my hands are already mangled
and i'm bleeding somewhere
i can feel it i just can't see it
i don't know how i got here
i don't know why I'm here
i just am

maybe i did this to myself
maybe this is the grave i dug for myself
and the devil helped pour the dirt over me
maybe that's why my lungs burn
i'm being suffocated by my own hands that
look very similarly to his

maybe this wasn't my fault
something led me here
something or someone that looked good
smelled good
tasted good

Grow Wild

felt good
or maybe something pushed me
which explains the way my bones ache
and crack when i move

something from the darkness hisses at me
"stop moving."

it is not quiet here
no it is so much louder here
and there's just one voice
but he's telling me so many different things at one time
my head is splintering
my ears are ringing
my nose is bleeding
please someone help me

HE IS LYING TO YOU
DO NOT BELIEVE HIM

there!
i see it
it looks like the crescent of a moon
or the sun split in half as it begins to rise

COME HERE
YOU CAN MOVE
TRUST ME
YOU CAN MOVE

maybe i'm numb
or maybe my bones have started to mend

the growth

but HE is right
i can move and
so i do
i am slow

IT'S OKAY
PLEASE TAKE YOUR TIME
IT IS NOT A RACE

but i am moving
and that's all that matters

i stumble

LET ME HELP YOU

suddenly
i am met by the moon and the sun all at once
i am set alight!
this is a fire
this is a cliffside lighthouse
this is color
i am warm
and i am healing
and i am no longer scared
i am no longer lost
i am no longer surrounded by darkness
but by

MY LIGHT
I WILL NOT LEAVE YOU IN THIS DARK
I HAVE FOUND YOU

Grow Wild

I WAS LOOKING FOR YOU EVERYWHERE
LET'S GO HOME

The Light helps me to my feet
no longer broken
and takes my hands
no longer mangled
and guides me back home

the growth

i am learning
what it's like to take up space.
i am allowing myself to expand
and not apologizing for it.

Grow Wild

therapeutic is the way
i make art out of my tragedy

the growth

daughter
you are worth more than where his hands touch you

Grow Wild

this is my body
not his or his or his
but His and mine
and it is a temple

the growth

God moves quietly
all the time
He is whispers
and breezes through leaves
and the subtle shifting of sand

Grow Wild

naming the demon that is hurting you most
breaks its hold over you
snaps its fingers in half
pushes it off your shoulders
already you feel so much lighter

the growth

God is quiet in the way that He
lays the path in front of me
it is hard to keep my heart from running ahead of Him
but He is also good in the way that He
urges it back between my ribs
"stay here for just a little longer,"
He murmurs and i feel His voice rumble through
the inner workings of my bones
"I promise we're almost there."

Grow Wild

when you look at a plant
you don't notice it
but it's always growing
people are like that
even if you don't notice it
you are always growing

the growth

the world is our oyster
look at everything you haven't seen yet
this road that stretches forever
God's footsteps go before you
all you have to do is follow

Grow Wild

He crashes like the waves against cliffside
splintering me into pieces
and i scramble to keep it all together
but it sifts through my fingers like sand
He tells me to leave it
"I have something so much better for you,"
His promise is a soft whisper
the breeze that tickles my ears and the back of my neck
i am at peace
move in my being like the ocean that You are

the growth

i have been a troubled sheep
with daunting fears and mounting anxieties
but now i find peace
my Shepherd leads me beside still waters
lays me down in quiet pastures
and the Holy Spirit says welcome

Grow Wild

God weeps today
and His tears bring greener grass,
deeper roots,
sweeter smelling air.

the growth

BECAUSE THE CREATOR OF THE UNIVERSE
HAS ALSO CREATED YOU
HIS EXISTENCE LIVES IN YOUR EVERYTHING
THE CAREFUL PLACEMENT OF EACH FRECKLE
THE CURVES OF YOUR FINGERPRINTS
THE SINKING DEPTHS OF YOUR EYES
HOW MUCH MORE PROOF DO YOU NEED?

Grow Wild

honey
let me tell you a secret
you are kissed by a God
a God whose love resembles galaxies
and sunsets
stretched vast
painted recklessly with color

but void tells me otherwise
and it echoes
and it is so loud

baby
let me show you His secret
the freckles on your face
the oceanic waves of your fingerprints
the bend in your knees
the ever so light step of your feet
this is where He's kissed you

the growth

the sun sinks below the horizon
and we are reminded
we are the golden children of God

Grow Wild

WHAT IS IT LIKE TO BE WOMAN
powerful
and strong
we can carry our own weight
WHAT IS IT LIKE TO BE WOMAN
well, what is it like to be Atlas?

the growth

she is headstrong
full of fire and made of lightning
watch her move the biggest mountains with her small hands

Grow Wild

i know what
God's heart feels like
it beats inside
my chest

the growth

tidal waves that crash hard into my chest
leave me breathless
gripping at the cliffside for help i am scared to drown
but God says take my hand
and i will pull you to your feet
keep you from falling over the edge

Grow Wild

He is in the uneven microscopic
etchings of my bones
interwoven around the spindles of my veins
He is my blood flow
and the oxygen in my lungs
He is the wood in my belly
that kindles the fire in my chest
and the supernova that explodes behind my eyes.
He is the specific curves of my hair,
the freckles dusted on my skin,
and the bending joints of my fingers.
He is everything i am.
i am everything He is.

if i am to imagine god
He would be golden hour
His kiss to earth
soft sunlight and illuminated skies
i can see the way His fingers drag colors through the clouds
pink blue purple orange
how can this not be god?
tell me where He doesn't exist
and i'll touch it and tell you the specific way that He does
in the carvings of tree bark
ringlets of age from when He spoke them into existence
in the jagged mountain ridges
giants made of rock with hands that stretch towards His heaven
in the careful rhythm of the ocean
deep blue symphonies that pull and push
sing and dance
in the way leaves shake
shimmying hips when His wind
His higher breath
whispers through them
and how can He not exist in the people?
the specific design of jawline
collar bone
shoulder blades that mimic His angels' wings
whispers of His traces in the hair
the skin
birthmarks
physical representations of His fingerprints
look into any one being's eyes and you'll see
His entirety

Grow Wild

His majesty
a greater expanse than any cosmic space around this planet
and you will sit here and tell me He does not exist?
darling,
He exists in you
telling yourself He does not exist is
like telling yourself that you don't exist.
it just doesn't make sense

the growth

God's love is a natural disaster
it dismantles buildings
and beats walls into dust
God's love swallows my flesh whole
pulls me into its depths
and washes me clean
its waves whisper and murmur to me
CHILD, I LOVE YOU ANYWAY

Grow Wild

the devil is in my head
i know his voice
chaotic and cacophonous violin strings
thick and heavy honey molasses
and wasp stings and crooked yellow teeth
and
he leaves me thirsty
my body is living in a desert
cracked dry skin
empty chest where water once flowed
parched lips
there is dirt underneath my fingernails from all the digging that
I'm doing
because i don't want to be thirsty
i'm trying to find the water
do you believe me?

WAIT
LISTEN
STOP DIGGING FOR A MINUTE
ALL THIS SCRATCHING IS MAKING YOU BLEED, DAUGHTER
YOU ARE SPILLING YOURSELF UNNECESSARY

it's hard to hear You over him
he is screaming at me
make him stop make him stop

HUSH
STOP TALKING AND JUST LISTEN

the growth

silence

a whisper
then

water

first dripping
then gushing
then flowing
it comes in heavenly rain

OPEN UP LITTLE ONE

and my ribs fall out of my chest
skeleton gives way to my emptiness
while this loving and living water floods its cavity
i can't hear him anymore
i am no longer thirsty
i am restored

she is soft
made of clay with His fingerprints
and He is ever-molding her
ever-shaping her
sometimes it hurts
but it is always Good.

"Here,"
He says
and places her on His display
for everyone to see.
"Look at all these things I have made her to be."gentle heart
brave heart
sometimes she has thunderstorms in her head and lightning in her
chest
"But,"
He says
"she is safe.
She is secure.
She is courage."

she likes to run
and can't seem to sit still
"I have made her to dance,"
He says
"dance on wild feet
and turning hips
and whipping hair.
My song is in her bones."

the growth

her hands are nimble
thin and long fingers
and everything she does is
"Intentional,"
He says
"She creates,
takes things broken and fashions them into new."
soft hands
trying so hard to hold the weak, the scared, the hurt
all of it hers and everyone else's
"But she forgets that it is not hers to hold,"
He says.

"Look at her,"
He says
"She is beautiful because I have made her that way,
long legs and crooked jaw and
crow hair and blue eyes.
All these things I made and
they are good.
She is good.
And I am proud,"
He says.

Grow Wild

bend like i am a skeleton tree and
He is the wind.
my creaking wood aching for release.

when someone dies in new orleans,
people hold funeral marches.
black and white flood the streets
and trumpets sing in mourning.
sometimes it feels like this in my bones.

towards the end of these funeral marches
grieving turns to celebration.
this singing does not mean death anymore but life
and confetti swirls like unraveling tornadoes of pain.
sometimes it feels like this in my bones
when Jesus calls to me.

gospel choir voices
and thick molasses guitar notes
harmonize with His voice
Lay It All Down.
Lay It All Down.

and i fall to my knees
there is pulling on my being
like these voices, THIS VOICE IS
tugging me into surrender.
there is no doubt with the Holy Spirit
a child can recognize her own Father's touch.

the growth

and the funeral marches on
but a funeral for what i once was

YOU ARE REDEEMED

my bones are singing
redemption
howling like trumpets

lay it all down
bury my knees in the soil of His grace
and take root

Grow Wild

look at it

look at everything you've championed little one

look at all the mountains you climbed

all the canyons you wandered through

the deserts that drained you of all your water

that cracked your skin into tectonic plates

the thunderstorms and lightning that shook earthquakes in your head

the fires that burned through your bones

but look at the way you conquered them

look at the way you reared My sword with trembling hands

and carved your demons to pieces

at the way you gathered My light and love to ease and cool your burns

to water your heart

to grow your soul

little one, look at the way you danced

kicking up and shaking off the dust

speaking life against the death with the symphonies in your feet

you harnessed the sun and gave its shine to the shadows

from dry bones to muscles and tissue and the strongest kick drum heartbeat

little one, just look at how far you've come

the growth

those hands were fires
spreading flames and consuming every inch of me
burning my skin and kissing me with a mouth of Death
for awhile i forgot what the color of my skin looked like
i have been colored black from soot and there was ash in my hair
and i couldn't breathe
my lungs were screaming
my bones crumbled into smoke and dust when touched

from fire and ashes come

restoration
renewal
rebirth
regrowth

this Higher Wind breathes air into my chest
He clears the ruin with His whispers and i am clean
this Living Water flows rapids through my veins and bones and
blood
and suddenly i am alive

Grow Wild

can you see it?

where fingerprints were, flowers sprout

with small petals, they stretch their faces to His Sun and

THRIVE

vines curl tight around my arms and legs and ivy crawls down my
spine and i am colored in

columbines

roses

lilies

orchids

tulips

poppies

there is a garden in my chest

there is a garden on

my body

is a garden

His garden

loved

nurtured

made new

the growth

there is a garden in my chest.
it is small but He waters it every day
with boundless grace and love.
the flowers,
i feel them,
tangled around the bones of my rib cage.
they tickle the walls of my stomach
and brush petals against the heavy beating of my heart.
their roots reach my toes,
curl around the soles of my feet.
you know,
for a long time
i thought this soil dry
and empty
but He told me otherwise,
buried His hands in the dirt and
pulled up a green I'd never seen before.
"This," He said to me,
"Is what I made you to be."
I feel them,
the flowers.
when i left,
they were barely anything but buds
and now
they are growing,
reaching heights new and foreign to me.
and now He says to me,
"Grow wild, my child."

* 9 7 8 1 6 6 6 7 1 9 4 7 5 *